WEATHER
Snow

by Ann Herriges

BLASTOFF! READERS 3

BELLWETHER MEDIA · MINNEAPOLIS, MN

Note to Librarians, Teachers, and Parents:

Blastoff! Readers are carefully developed by literacy experts and combine standards-based content with developmentally-appropriate text.

Level 1 provides the most support through repetition of high-frequency words, light text, predictable sentence patterns, and strong visual support.

Level 2 offers early readers a bit more challenge through varied simple sentences, increased text load, and less repetition of high frequency words.

Level 3 advances early-fluent readers toward fluency through increased text and concept load, less reliance on visuals, longer sentences, and more literary language.

Level 4 builds reading stamina by providing more text per page, increased use of punctuation, greater variation in sentence patterns, and increasingly challenging vocabulary.

Level 5 encourages children to move from "learning to read" to "reading to learn" by providing even more text, varied writing styles, and less familiar topics.

Whichever book is right for your reader, Blastoff! Readers are the perfect books to build confidence and encourage a love of reading that will last a lifetime!

This edition first published in 2010 by Bellwether Media, Inc.

No part of this publication may be reproduced in whole or in part without written permission of the publisher. For information regarding permission, write to Bellwether Media, Inc., Attention: Permissions Department, 5357 Penn Avenue South, Minneapolis, MN 55419.

Library of Congress Cataloging-in-Publication Data
Herriges, Ann.
  Snow / by Ann Herriges.
    p. cm. — (Blastoff! readers) (Weather)
  Summary: "Simple text and supportive images introduce beginning readers to the characteristics of snow. Intended for students in kindergarten through third grade."
  Includes bibliographical references and index.
  ISBN-13: 978-1-60014-397-7 (paperback : alk. paper)
  1. Snow—Juvenile literature. 2. Weather—Juvenile literature. I. Title. II. Series.

QC926.37.H47 2007
551.57'84—dc22

2006000619

Table of Contents

Snow is ice that falls from **clouds**.
Snow falls when the air is
very cold.

Snowflakes form high inside a cloud.
They start as tiny ice **crystals**.

The ice crystals grow bigger
and heavier. They fall
through the cloud.

The ice crystals smash into each other. When they stick together they form bigger snowflakes.

Most snowflakes have six sides.
They come in many shapes.

This snowflake has thin **branches**. It looks like a star.

This snowflake has
thick branches.

This snowflake has almost
no branches at all.

These snowflakes are a **jumble** of ice crystals.

Every snowflake is different.

Sometimes big, fluffy snowflakes fall to the ground. This snow is wet and heavy.

Other times small, crisp snowflakes fall to the ground. This snow is light and powdery.

Snow that falls in a **flurry** stops and starts again. A flurry does not bring much snow.

Snow falls fast during a snowstorm. The snow can really pile up!

The biggest snowstorms are **blizzards**. Strong winds blow snow around so much that it is hard to see.

The air becomes icy cold. It is dangerous to be outside during a blizzard.

Snow covers the ground after a snowstorm. Sometimes winds push the snow into huge **drifts**.

The snow stays until warm
weather melts it away.

Glossary

blizzard—a snowstorm with strong winds, heavy snow, and cold temperatures

branches—arms or smaller parts of something larger

cloud—tiny drops of water or crystals of ice that float together in the air

crystal—a solid that has a pattern of many flat sides; an ice crystal is water frozen into a six-sided solid.

drift—a pile of snow made by the wind

flurry—a snow shower that stops and starts

jumble—a messy mix of things

To Learn More

AT THE LIBRARY

Gibbons, Gail. *Weather Words and What They Mean*. New York: Holiday House, 1990.

Martin, Jacqueline Briggs. *Snowflake Bentley*. Boston: Houghton Mifflin, 1998.

Shulevitz, Uri. *Snow*. New York: Farrar Straus Giroux, 1998.

Waldman, Neil. *The Snowflake: A Water Cycle Story*. Brookfield, Conn.: Millbrook Press, 2003.

ON THE WEB

Learning more about the weather is as easy as 1, 2, 3.

1. Go to www.factsurfer.com

2. Enter "weather" into search box.

3. Click the "Surf" button and you will see a list of related web sites.

With factsurfer.com, finding more information is just a click away.

Index

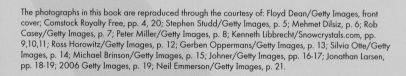
The photographs in this book are reproduced through the courtesy of: Floyd Dean/Getty Images, front cover; Comstock Royalty Free, pp. 4, 20; Stephen Studd/Getty Images, p. 5; Mehmet Dilsiz, p. 6; Rob Casey/Getty Images, p. 7; Peter Miller/Getty Images, p. 8; Kenneth Libbrecht/Snowcrystals.com, pp. 9,10,11; Ross Horowitz/Getty Images, p. 12; Gerben Oppermans/Getty Images, p. 13; Silvia Otte/Getty Images, p. 14; Michael Brinson/Getty Images, p. 15; Johner/Getty Images, pp. 16-17; Jonathan Larsen, pp. 18-19; 2006 Getty Images, p. 19; Neil Emmerson/Getty Images, p. 21.